D1454854

DATE DUE

? '92

HIGH IMPACT TEACHING

Strategies for
Educating
Minority Youth

Thomas J. Brown

UNIVERSITY
PRESS OF
AMERICA

Lanham • New York • London

Copyright © 1988 by

University Press of America,® Inc.

4720 Boston Way
Lanham, MD 20706

3 Henrietta Street
London WC2E 8LU England

British Cataloging in Publication Information Available

Library of Congress Cataloging-in-Publication Data

Brown, Thomas J., 1933– .
High impact teaching : strategies for educating minority youth /
Thomas J. Brown.
p. cm.
Bibliography: p.
1. Minorities—Education—United States. 2. Motivation in
education. 3. Teaching. 4. Academic achievement. I. Title.
LC3731.B72   1988
371.97'00973—dc 19   88–1388 CIP
ISBN 0–8191–6889–0 (alk. paper)
ISBN 0–8191–6890–4 (pbk. : alk. paper)

All University Press of America books are produced on acid-free
paper which exceeds the minimum standards set by the National
Historical Publications and Records Commission.

To those who dare to see the unique
challenges to teaching as opportunities
to shape the future of the world.

ACKNOWLEDGEMENTS

My most sincere appreciation is being expressed to:

My wife, Joyce, for assistance in proofreading and for encouragement.

My daughter, Glynis, for incorporating many of these strategies into her student teaching experience.

My son, Daryl, whose perseverance allowed him to overcome many of the inequities faced on a predominantly white university campus.

My friend and colleague, Mrs. Joanne Parton, for typing this manuscript.

My colleagues at the Talbott Springs Elementary School who have made many of these ideas a permanent part of their teaching repertoire.

CONTENTS

PREFACE

This handbook is designed specifically to assist educational practitioners in responding more effectively to the challenge of interrupting the cycle of minority underachievement. For those charged with the responsibility of guiding learning experiences for culturally diverse student population, it is the most difficult challenge they must face. Recognition of that fact has been the major impetus behind this effort.

The national conference on Educating Black Children has played an important role in arousing the conscience of this country's educators and mobilizing many essential resources for the tasks which must be accomplished in the future. Accompanying the tremendous amount of enthusiasm generated through this conference was absolute proof that the knowledge and skill necessary to ensure that all students learn at levels commensurate with their potential already exist and are being used effectively in various parts of the country.

What needs to be accomplished at this point is an efficient process for disseminating what works to those who are committed to engaging in more productive educational exchanges with youth. By achieving this objective, we will have established a support system that encourages teachers to stand on the shoulders of giants. This effort is directed toward that end. Its most significant attribute may be the potential to generate and sustain maximum increases in academic achievement from a minimal amount of educational reform.

Thomas J. Brown

Columbia, Maryland
August, 1987

FOREWORD

Our experience of almost ten years of assisting school districts to improve educational opportunities for minority students has clearly demonstrated the difficulties faced by even the best intentioned teachers. Traditionally educated teachers have difficulty in establishing a productive educational environment of mutual respect and comfort when faced with students of minority cultures and distinct socio-economic backgrounds. Tom Brown is an educational leader who has demonstrated his ability to assist teachers in establishing a warm and challenging educational environment for all students. In his earlier work, <u>Teaching Minorities More Effectively: A Model for Educators</u>, he addressed issues of student motivation, classroom behavior and student/teacher interaction with concrete examples that only an educator truly familiar with today's classroom could have produced.

In this new handbook, <u>High Impact Teaching: Strategies for Educating Minority Youth</u>, Mr. Brown is once again concerned with assisting educators to be successful in their efforts to break the cycle of minority underachievement. His objective is to assist educators both white and Black to better understand the pervasiveness of white middle class culture in our classrooms. He helps teachers to see that taking white middle class culture for granted can have a strongly negative effect on students from other cultures and socio-economic classes. Mr. Brown not only helps us to better understand our own class biases, but provides us with concrete examples of how we can overcome them in our classrooms. Reminding us that we should start with the students, their culture and their individual interests, he provides us with activities that can help teachers to gain more information about their students while assisting them to practice higher order thinking skills.

While Tom Brown grapples with complex issues of class and culture, he never loses sight of the classroom and never makes a suggestion without providing us with some concrete strategies for the classroom. He helps us to better understand how to respect our students and to encourage our students to respect themselves. Tom Brown provides us with information and techniques that will help us to stimulate student motivation and enhance their interest in the learning process. Finally, he provides us with a self assessment tool that we can use to monitor our own efforts to increase minority student achievement.

Sheryl Denbo

(Sheryl Denbo is Executive Director of The Mid-Atlantic Equity Center, a regional race, sex and national origin desegregation center affiliated with the School of Education at The American University)

CHAPTER ONE

INTRODUCTION

While the strategies presented in this handbook have been found to produce amazing results with all children, their most significant impact occurs among minority students. Minorities may be defined as those who possess traits, characteristics, and other lifeways that run counter to those of the dominant culture in our society. The failure of students from these groups to achieve academically is a well documented reality. Recognition of this fact has figured prominently in educational planning for the past thirty years. That period has given rise to many theories which have been advanced as explanations for this lack of achievement. Unfortunately, none of them has resulted in recommendations for substantial modifications in our educational exchanges with youth.

Bereiter groups these theories explaining the lack of academic achievement by minorities into five categories.[1] Each, when examined carefully, reflects a number of factors indigenous to minority lifeways that inhibits academic growth in the school setting. This assertion is true partially because schools are not designed for minorities, and partially because our methods of interacting with students are not sufficiently responsive to ethnically, economically, and racially diverse populations. In many cases, minority students are expected to achieve less; thus, they are afforded fewer legitimate opportunities to become actively engaged in the learning process. In short, they are taught less effectively than those students whose lifestyles more nearly approximate the "Great American Dream." When the lack of academic achievement by minorities is examined from this perspective, reasons seldom addressed by educators are brought more clearly into focus.

A PERSPECTIVE ON MOTIVATION

Motivation may be thought of as the general energizing syndrome that initiates, sustains, and regulates various kinds of activity. While there are many conflicting theories concerning how it operates, the fact that it is a variable that affects learning enjoys universal agreement. Motivation can be used as a partial explanation for why some individuals soar to positions of prominence while others, with similar intellectual endowments, never rise above mediocrity. Two logical conclusions that may be drawn from this observation are:

- Individuals are motivated for different reasons and by different stimuli.

2

- What may cause one individual or group to become highly motivated to achieve may have no observable influence on another.

For many students who are making only marginal progress, the reason most often thought to be responsible is their lack of motivation to achieve. This kind of reasoning by teachers seems to prevail regardless of the students' degree of interest in and perceived relevance of the learning tasks. Teacher assumptions that minorities are lacking in motivation to achieve are reinforced when these students do not respond enthusiastically to opportunities for acquiring those skills which curriculum builders believe are essential to a productive way of life.

A major premise upon which the ideas presented through this handbook are based is that the motivational process is the critical determinant that forecasts success or failure in the teaching endeavor. It is for teachers THE FIRST AND GREAT COMMANDMENT. Its critical importance is derived partially from the fact that it must be handled at the very outset of a learning experience, and partially from its potential to influence all that follows.[2]

Keeping students highly motivated to achieve is one of the more difficult challenges teachers will encounter. That challenge is made even more difficult by the rapid growth in ethnic, racial, and economic diversity within a given school population. The degree of success experienced by teachers is, to a large extent, dependent upon their understanding of how culture influences cognition.

Axiology, the study of value systems, and epistemology, the study of the nature of learning and the bases for knowledge, indicate that differences reflected through lifeways hold important implications for enhancing the educative process. Dr. Edward Nichols, in a presentation to mid-level managers from the Department of Health, Education, and Welfare, pointed out the necessity for understanding the various value orientations of a culturally diverse work force.[3] He indicated that the value systems of middle-class white Americans (Euro-American) are based on relationships of individuals to objects. The term "OBJECTS" takes on multiple meanings including abstract qualities. By contrast, the value orientations of Blacks and Hispanics are based on relationships of individuals to individuals. At the risk of over simplifying a set of complex sociological dynamics, one could assume that substantial differences in values and valuing would exist among these groups. In reality, those differences do exist. However, it is when some of these values are perceived as being better than others that creates problems in the work place.

Differences in values orientation, which must be recognized by successful managers of multi-ethnic work forces, should be of no lesser importance to teachers of culturally-diverse student populations. While it is true that values form the bases for many real-life decisions, they are neither right nor wrong; they simply exist in all of us. Two clear messages for teachers that could be extracted from the Nichols presentation are:

- Differences should not only be tolerated, they should be affirmed.

- It is through the affirmation of differences that individuals' worth is acknowledged.

4

Epistemological considerations in teaching must transcend what have come to be known as learning styles. This is not to suggest that attempts to accommodate a variety of learning styles are not essential, but rather to indicate that an understanding of the concepts which gave rise to learning styles theory is even more crucial. The basis for knowledge that accompanies the Euro-American value system is characterized by Dr. Nichols as counting and measuring.[4] These learners perceive a necessity for knowing all of the parts that combine to form the whole and each step of the process that results in a product. Their approach to learning is rational, logical, symbolic, and analytic. By comparison, Blacks and Hispanics are more likely to learn through spatial, analogic, holistic, and intuitive thought processes. Adequate understanding of the implications for teaching arising from epistemological considerations serves to remind us that students learn not only for different reasons, but they learn in different ways.

In the chapters that follow, a framework for designing high impact teaching strategies for culturally diverse student populations will be presented. Rationale for their use and guiding principles to be followed are included to facilitate implementation.

CHAPTER ONE   ENDNOTES

[1]Carl Bereiter, "The Changing Face of Educational Dis-
advantagement," <u>Phi Delta Kappan</u>, LXVI (April, 1985),
pp. 538-541.

[2]Thomas J. Brown, <u>Teaching Minorities More Effec-
tively</u>, (Lanham, MD: University Press of America, Inc.,
1986), p. 57.

[3]Edward Nichols, Comments made at a symposium on
mid-level management in Marriottsville, MD in October,
1986.

[4]Ibid.

CHAPTER TWO

ESTABLISHING AND MAINTAINING
AN ATMOSPHERE OF
MUTUAL RESPECT

Just because each of us has achieved the right to be called TEACHER, there are no assurances that we will command respect from all students. Respect must be earned. The discussion that follows provides a blueprint for displaying teacher attitudes and behaviors from which mutual respect is most likely to emerge. While some of the points presented are controversial, the controversy arises from an acceptance or rejection of the following postulates:

TEACHING IS INTERACTION THAT
FACILITATES LEARNING.

DIFFERENCES MUST NOT ONLY BE TOLERATED, THEY MUST BE AFFIRMED.

VALUES ARE NEITHER RIGHT NOR WRONG; THEY SIMPLY EXIST IN ALL OF US.

FREEDOM TO CHOOSE IS ONE OF THE MOST PRECIOUS RIGHTS WE HAVE.

THOSE WHO DARE TO TEACH MUST NEVER CEASE TO LEARN.

Teachers who subscribe to these five postulates have little difficulty establishing and maintaining an atmosphere of mutual respect. The excerpts from classroom realities included in this chapter demonstrate how acceptance of the first postulate encourages agreement with the others. A recurring theme central to each of these excerpts is IF YOU CAN'T INTERACT WITH THEM, YOU CAN'T TEACH THEM.

TEACHING IS INTERACTION THAT
FACILITATES LEARNING.

It is obvious that teaching, with all its ramifications, is perceived in a variety of ways. Implicit in those perceptions are assumptions regarding how it can be accomplished most effectively. When reduced to its essence, it is interaction that facilitates learning. What should be understood from this analysis is that any attitude or behavior that has an adverse effect on teacher/student interaction has a similar effect on learning. If our interaction with students is not humanly enhancing, the likelihood of establishing and maintaining the kind of relationship that supports teaching and learning is reduced significantly.

A guiding principle that should govern our educational exchanges with youth is IF YOU CAN'T INTERACT WITH THEM, YOU CAN'T TEACH THEM.

DIFFERENCES MUST NOT ONLY BE TOLERATED,
THEY MUST BE
AFFIRMED.

In a culturally pluralistic society, recognizing differences is an inescapable obligation. It is through the affirmation of differences that individuals' self-worth is acknowledged. However, differences should serve only to make distinctions, not to determine inherent value.

Interacting with students whose dominant speech patterns reflect variant dialects of English is a challenge most teachers will have to face. Educators who are committed to affirming differences have developed strategies that utilize what students already know to help them acquire the skills they want them to learn. This can be accomplished without compromising either the teacher's obligation to have all students demonstrate proficiency in speaking and writing the prestige dialect or the kind of relationship necessary for meaningful interaction to occur. Any efforts directed toward this end must begin with teacher acceptance of variant dialects of English as legitimate aspects of this nation's cultural heritage. Their legitimacy rests on the following facts:

- They satisfy the requirements for mutual intelligibility.

- They are systematic.

- They represent for some the only means of communication known.

The point was made earlier in this writing that if minorities are to enjoy the kinds of benefits that should accrue from schooling, educators must devise strategies which allow their culture to figure prominently in the learning process. Handling variant dialects of English presents numerous opportunities to test this theory. Unfortunately, far too many educators fail to use those opportunities in ways that are humanly enhancing and educationally enriching.

Teachers who have launched vigorous campaigns to eradicate the use of variant dialects of English from school settings are not only fighting a losing battle, they are erecting barriers to meaningful interaction which are extremely difficult to remove. When students are told constantly that their verb forms are incorrect, their syntax is awkward: their modifiers are misplaced, or their speech is unacceptable for school, they decide that the risks associated with attempts to communicate with teachers outweigh the benefits. This decision results in limited interaction with teachers and ultimately, limited opportunities to engage actively in planned learning experiences. Those who become willing participants in these counterproductive campaigns need to be reminded that IF YOU CAN'T INTERACT WITH THEM, YOU CAN'T TEACH THEM.

Now let's examine a pedagogically sound approach that utilizes what students already know to assist them in acquiring the skills we want to teach. Teachers who possess an adequate understanding of the structure of American English recognize that there are many dialectical variants in existence. They also recognize that most native speakers of variant dialects speak them fluently and in accordance with the linguistic structure upon which they are founded. Because these teachers have reached this level of enlightenment, they perceive these variations not as the prestige dialect spoken incorrectly, but rather as structurally different dialects. It is essential that students view this push toward facility with the prestige dialect as an attempt to have them acquire another

13

way of communicating as opposed to a campaign to eradicate the one they are using.

An effective way to accomplish this is through comparative analyses and progressive differentiations between the dialects under study. However, this can be achieved only when teachers possess a working knowledge of the structure of both dialects. The accuracy of the translations by teachers is crucial to the successful implementation of this approach. In one variant dialect. "She be's jogging" and "She jogging" convey significantly different messages. "She be's jogging" is a dialectical variant of the habitual tense verb form while "She jogging" is a variant of the present tense verb form. An accurate comparative analysis would indicate the differences between equivalent forms:

"She be's jogging." = She jogs.

"She jogging." = She is jogging.

When accurate translations are made by teachers, students can be expected to switch codes with relative ease. Much of the effectiveness of this approach is realized because students see it as being additive rather than subtractive. They see themselves as gaining a new dialect without having to give up what is already theirs.

It is conceivable that the diversity of your school's student population may encompass several different variant dialects of English. In these cases, a dominant dialect will emerge. Students' need to conform allows them to engage in this kind of compromise rather painlessly. By the end of the second week of school, you can assume that the dialect being spoken is familiar to all students who do not use the prestige dialect consistently.

Learning the dialect in vogue can be accomplished by most teachers in four easy steps:

1. Collect speech samples from unstructured conversations in sufficient quantity to ensure that all tenses utilized are included. Pure samples must be used, and they are most easily obtained by listening to student conversations in the cafeteria or on the playground. Samples obtained from conversations involving students and teachers are usually contaminated by students' attempts to speak in a manner thought to be more nearly acceptable.

2. Analyze the samples within the context used so that accurate understanding can be achieved. When in doubt, ask the students. Remember that while the prestige dialect is not used by these students in expressive language, it is an important part of their receptive language facility. The very fact that you care enough to ask does a lot to establish mutual respect.

3. Translate to the prestige dialect noting the differences in linguistic structure.

4. Write a grammar for the variant dialect. This is for your own enrichment. The students have already mastered it.

Armed with this newly-acquired knowledge and firmly committed to defending students' right to choose, your chances of having all of them demonstrate proficiency in English are increased significantly. It is important to emphasize that the acquisition of the prestige dialect means that they have two languages at their command and the right to choose when either is more appropriate for a given set of circumstances. As usual, that choice should be based on a careful analysis of benefits and consequences. Under these conditions, enthusiasm for learning becomes the rule rather than the exception.

In a study entitled, "Copying with the Burden of Acting White." Fordham and Ogbu addressed a number of issues associated with deliberate attempts by Blacks to limit academic success for themselves and other Blacks.[1] Many of those issues are muted by the guiding principles and specific strategies set forth in this handbook. To use these principles effectively is to confront what Kunjufu describes as the conspiracy against black males.[2]

VALUES ARE NEITHER RIGHT NOR WRONG;
THEY SIMPLY EXIST IN ALL OF US.

The sharing of middle-class values among teachers is common throughout the country. However, the same cannot be said for student populations. Cultural diversity, by definition, implies differences in values and valuing. When encountered, these differences should be treated as factors indigenous to various ways of life rather than ideas and practices which are inherently of less worth.

Dealing with a variety of ideas and beliefs that may run counter to those held by many mainstream-Americans is another of those inescapable realities for teachers of culturally diverse student populations. These different beliefs form the basis for many real-life decisions. Unfortunately, this simple truth is not always taken into account by teachers. Ed Smith, in the book - <u>BLACK STUDENTS IN INTERRACIAL SCHOOLS</u> - indicated that one professor went so far as to say that the reason non-Anglo cultures are not taken seriously is that the schools have "culturally deficient educators" trying to teach culturally different students.[3] The following story was used to illustrate how we allow our own values to color perceptions of the actions of others:

> A Westerner who sees an Oriental friend putting a bowl of rice on his grandfather's grave says, "When will your grandfather get up to eat the rice?" His friend replied, "At the same time that your grandfather gets up to smell the flowers you put on his grave."[4]

Values emerge from conscious decisions and choices. To

denegrate those values we find to be personally affronting is to strain the kind of relationship needed to support meaningful interaction. Any influence we have on changing students' values should follow from our efforts to present a variety of options and to encourage the making of more appropriate choices based on an analysis of benefits and consequences. Remember, IF WE CAN'T INTERACT WITH THEM, WE CAN'T TEACH THEM.

FREEDOM TO CHOOSE IS ONE OF THE MOST
PRECIOUS RIGHTS WE HAVE.

The right to exercise freedom of choice should be protected for children and adults with equal vigor. Educational practitioners must realize that students cannot be forced to conform with their desires. Even the most liberal interpretation of "in loco parentis" does not justify the quest for absolute control over students. That attitude, when exhibited by teachers or administrators, is both self-serving and self-defeating. To use a jaded analogy, it's much like trying to teach a pig to whistle. You invariably experience failure, and you irritate the pig in the process. A more realistic approach is to encourage students to make appropriate choices based on a range of consequences. This suggests that our expectations for students' behavior and a range of consequences for nonconformance should be understood by all.

Because of the limited amount of success experienced by a large number of teachers in having all students recognize the immediate impact made on their lives by the acquisition of certain skills, much of their interaction is relegated to managing behavior. Since this is a reality of classroom life that occurs with alarming regularity, the major objective to be accomplished should be emphasized. WE MANAGE BEHAVIOR IN ORDER TO ENHANCE OPPORTUNITIES FOR INTERACTION THAT FACILITATES LEARNING. When behavior management is viewed from this perspective, teachers are more inclined to analyze the impact of their interventions on students' motivation to achieve. However, because attempts at managing behavior are inspired by what teachers perceive as inappropriate acts, additional cautions are warranted.

Moralizing about student behaviors and describing those behaviors in demeaning terms create impediments to meaningful interaction that are difficult to overcome. It must be recognized that many of the same behaviors that are inappropriate for the school setting are accepted, even celebrated, in a large number of homes. They are displayed consistently by parents and other relatives. To have those behaviors described as morally wrong or demeaned in any way is perceived often by students as an attack on their family as well as their entire social structure. When feelings such as these are generated, students avoid interacting with teachers altogether. Remember, IF WE CAN'T INTERACT WITH THEM, WE CAN'T TEACH THEM. It is not our purpose to eradicate those behaviors that offend us. Our responsibility for student behavior begins and ends with encouraging them to make more appropriate choices based on an analysis of consequences. Any lasting changes in behavior that may result from this process should be considered bonus returns on our investment of time and energy.

Avoid getting into power struggles. Aside from the fact that teachers invariably lose, they diminish themselves in the process. To believe that we hold the power to force compliance with our demands is to be naive. Attempts to do so are open invitations for defiance.

A final caution is not to ignore unacceptable behavior. Students need and desire adult guidance. Once expectations have been established, the practice of ignoring unacceptable behavior serves only to send confusing messages about where limits are being drawn.

THOSE WHO DARE TO TEACH MUST
NEVER CEASE TO LEARN.

There is a need for educators to seek information about minority cultures from all available sources, verify the information obtained to form a knowledge base, and develop from that knowledge base a set of understandings that serves to modify many current teaching behaviors.

One irrefutable fact about learning is when students achieve at levels commensurate with potential, their culture figures prominently in the process. The influence of culture on cognition must never be overlooked. Those teachers who devise creative strategies for taking full advantage of what students already know are also committed to seeking information about how they live. These are the same teachers who produce significantly greater learning outcomes for all. The more you know about the students you teach, the more proficient you become at guiding their learning experiences.

Of all the conditions of learning recognized as such by educators, none is more essential to education that is truly multicultural than establishing and maintaining an atmosphere of mutual respect. The five postulates outlined in this chapter form the bedrock upon which mutual respect rests.

CHAPTER TWO

ENDNOTES

[1]Signithia Fordham and John U. Ogbu, "Black Students' School Success: Coping with the Burden of Acting White," The Urban Review, XVIII, (April, 1986), pp. 176-205.

[2]Jawanza Kunjufu, Countering the Conspiracy to Destroy Black Boys, Chicago; African American Images, 1985.

[3]Ed Smith, Black Students in Interracial Schools: A Guide for Students, Teachers, and Parents, (Garrett Park, MD: Garrett Park Press, 1980), p. 88.

[4]Ibid.

CHAPTER THREE

ESTABLISHING NEED TO KNOW

For many students, interest in learning is directly related to their perceived relevance of the learning tasks. They need to know how their existing lifestyles can be influenced by acquiring certain kinds of knowledge and skills. When a need to know is clear and present, efforts toward skills acquisition are more energetic. Evidence of this fact can be observed readily among students enrolled in classes such as driver education, swimming, and computer literacy. However, the kind of enthusiasm for learning exhibited by most students in these classes is not evident in other areas of the curriculum. This observation does not allude to the relative importance of the various curriculum areas, but rather the degree to which their importance is perceived by students.

The discussion that follows presents some important considerations for establishing student perceptions of relevance and some practical interventions directed toward achieving that end.

NEUTRALIZING FEELINGS OF EXCLUSION

It is impossible for teachers to predict accurately how the lives of individual students will be influenced by the acquisition of certain skills. In spite of this fact, many teachers find it necessary to try. These attempts very often are couched in statements of purpose for a given learning activity. The statements that follow are typical of those made by teachers at the very outset of a learning experience:

> "Today, we are going to examine some principles of thermodynamics. These concepts are critical for those of you aspiring to become engineers."

> "The purpose of today's lesson is to analyze the effects of purchasing imported goods on our nation's economy. This information will become extremely valuable to those who may be considering professions in banking, economic analysis, or financial planning."

> "Today, we are going to learn more about reading maps and graphs. These skills are essential for urban planners, geologists, and surveyors."

Implicit in such statements are assumptions about the kinds of impact acquiring certain skills should produce as well as the kinds of students that benefit most from their acquisition.

The argument can be made that an essential component of effective teaching is ensuring that students realize why they are being asked to engage in various learning activities. However, while teachers should play an important role in that process, students must arrive at the realization on their own. When this is achieved by each individual in the class, a major impediment to learning has been overcome.

It is reasonable to assume that the purposes for learning contained in curriculum guides and teachers' editions of many texts, as well as those created by experienced teachers, serve a useful purpose. While that assumption is partially correct, the extent of that usefulness is limited to the number of students whose motivation to achieve is enhanced. Because these purposes for learning relate almost exclusively to the lifestyles of middle-class Americans, many minority students perceive them as being irrelevant. The extent to which this occurs is the extent to which interference to learning has been introduced. Each occurrence provides a classic example of how an educational practice which is generally accepted as being sound can be counterproductive for minorities. Teachers who consistently state purposes for learning are unwittingly establishing legitimate escape routes for all students who find those purposes uninviting.

The point being emphasized here is that culture has a tremendous influence on cognition. This suggests that many legitimate reasons for learning seldom alluded to by teachers need to be celebrated in the classroom. For students who live in poorly-heated houses, reasons for learning some principles of thermodynamics are just as compelling as those held by students who aspire to become engineers. Because teachers have not been trained sufficiently to take full advantage of the influence of culture on cognition, a significant amount of learning potential for those who are culturally different is being sacrificed.

Ernest Boyer, in an address before the Council of Chief State School Officers, identified the major challenge educators must face as finding ways to help students see the connections between what we teach and how they live. This profound statement attests to the need for expanding our concept of multi-cultural education to include teaching strategies that utilize the knowledge and skills students have gained through a variety of lifeways. If minorities are to enjoy the kinds of benefits that should accrue from schooling, then educational practitioners must devise techniques which will allow their culture to figure prominently in the process.

To reduce feelings of exclusion and perceptions of irrelevance held by many minority students, teachers must make a conscious effort to have them realize that the material about to be taught will have some immediate impact on the lives of each individual in the class. An introductory statement such as the one that follows will facilitate that effort:

> "Each of you will be affected in some
> way by the skills and concepts about to
> be presented. This is true regardless of

who you are, where you live, how you manage lifestyle, and what values you embrace. Today, we will begin a study of_____."

This kind of introduction empowers all students to assume an active role in the learning experiences that have been planned. It is instrumental in generating open educational exchanges through which insights about teaching and learning can be gained. These exchanges flourish when students feel the security of a classroom that is psychologically safe and free of derision. Under these conditions, they are willing, even anxious, to share more information about themselves than we need to know. To maintain a productive level of discussion, we need only to ask the right questions and display genuine interest in their responses. Questions similar to those that follow elicit valuable information about students' reasons for learning:

- What activities take place in your home or community that require some knowledge of _____?

- How is your involvement in these activities made more effective by some knowledge of _____?

- How can a knowledge of_____ improve the quality of life for you and your relatives in other ways?

- How can the quality of life be diminished by not possessing this kind of knowledge?

This exercise has a very powerful impact on students' motivation to achieve. Its importance as a critical component of the introductory phase for a new unit of study cannot be overstated. The amount of information generated is increased substantially when Frank Lyman's model of THINK-PAIR-SHARE is utilized. This provides students with time to think and to share ideas in pairs or triads. After thirty to forty-five seconds, individual students may be recognized to share their experiences with the class. Participation by each student in the class is more likely to be realized if a process similar to that which has been outlined here is used. However time consuming it may be, it is an investment that pays huge dividends. If this investment of time and energy is not made at the very beginning of a learning experience, significantly more time and energy must be directed toward managing behavior.

RECOGNIZING THAT STUDENTS LEARN FOR DIFFERENT REASONS

The responses to questions relating to how certain knowledge and skills are utilized in real-life situations are clear indications that students learn many of the same things for a variety of reasons. One student's reason for wanting to acquire map skills may relate to a weekend job with Western Union. Another's reason may relate to a desire to plan an auto route for the family's pending cross-country tour. Still another reason may relate to a student's desire to earn a merit badge in scouting. Conceivably, the number of different reasons for learning may equal the number of students in the class. Teachers who insist on setting purposes for acquiring certain skills run the risk of sending subtle messages about which reasons for learning are of most worth. Because those purposes invariably relate to middle-class lifestyles, many legitimate reasons for learning are never mentioned. Students view this behavior as arising from teacher perceptions that their reasons for learning are unimportant. For the students who develop this attitude, motivation to engage in learning activities within the school setting is diminished.

RECOGNIZING CULTURAL DIFFERENCES

Activities, ideas, aspirations, and other bits of information pertaining to various ways of life will be brought out in these introductory discussions. In some instances, practices may be explained that, in our opinion, are deplorable. What each of us needs to keep in mind is that many of those practices are indigenous to a way of life.

Consider, for a moment, how one's motivation to achieve might be influenced by the following circumstances:

- Being either of seven children who lives with a single parent in a one-bedroom apartment

- Being a "squeegee kid" washing automobile windshields at a busy intersection to subsidize family income

- Living in a household with no heat for one week or each winter month

- Being a twelve-year old youngster with the responsibility of caring for five younger siblings from the time school is dismissed until midnight

These are descriptions of situations that exist throughout the nation. For educators, they emphasize contrasts in lifestyles. Perceptive teachers affirm those contrasts by recognizing that students who live in poorly-heated houses may have different reasons for wanting to learn some principles of thermodynamics from those whose homes are more comfortable.

EMPHASIZING THE IMPORTANCE OF LEARNING

Contrary to the opinions of some curriculum critics, much of the knowledge and many of the skills taught in schools improve the quality of life for all students. However, just as reasons for learning differ among culturally diverse student populations, learning outcomes influence their lifestyles in different ways. As professional educators, one of our obligations is to have all students realize that regardless of the lifestyle pursued, its quality is improved by the knowledge and skills acquired through active participation in the learning process.

CHAPTER FOUR

DISCOVERING WHAT STUDENTS
ALREADY KNOW

If we accept the conclusion that culture influences cognition, then we would expect students to be more knowledgeable about and express greater interest in those things which are indigenous to their lifestyles. Regardless of how those lifestyles may be perceived, they exert an incredible amount of influence on learning. Each generates a set of understandings as well as requirements for the acquisition of basic skills. While some of these lifestyles may seem completely foreign to us, students who embrace them come to school in possession of a body of knowledge that can be related in some way to anything we attempt to teach. The challenge for educators is to utilize what they already know in ways that will facilitate their acquiring those skills curriculum planners consider essential to a productive way of life.

Knowledge pertaining to global issues such as those listed below is critical to one's existence irrespective of culture:

- Communication Processes

- Decision-Making Processes

- Conflict Resolution

- Counting and Measuring

- Consumer Economics

- Health and Safety

Many student understandings related to these common strands may be inconsistent with those we are attempting to teach. However, establishing the fact that a relationship exists accomplishes several important purposes:

- It indicates clearly that the concepts being taught are not totally alien.

- It serves to expand cultural boundaries.

- It allows some assimilation to occur with minimal resistance.

Civilized societies have been found to exhibit more similarities than differences. This suggests that many commonalities among lifestyles are impervious to ethnic, racial, and economic diversity. For educators, these commonalities become the most productive points of departure for skills development and concept formation.

An effective way to solicit contributions indicating what students already know is through a process of creative problem solving. You may begin by having your class engage in brainstorming exercises designed to produce possible solutions for problems that affect the human condition. Whether the problems identified for this activity are real or contrived is inconsequential. However, it is important that they relate to either of those cross-cultural strands if our major purpose is to be served.

For maximum benefits to be derived from the brainstorming exercises, participation by each student is essential. All of the solutions recommended should be recorded on chart paper for future reference. After the students' suggestions have been exhausted, more detailed explanations may be offered by each contributor. At this point, you are ready to embark on a truly enriching teaching/learning experience. Each student present understands the connection between what is being taught and how he or she lives. More importantly, each understands that the acquisition of this knowledge can serve to improve the quality of life in a variety of ways.

Let's assume that you are about to introduce a new unit of study. Decide which of the cross-cultural strands is most closely related to the skills or concepts to be developed. To find out what kinds of knowledge the children already possess, have them propose solutions to problems such as these:

COMMUNICATION PROCESSES

- A small plane carrying a group of photographers over a section of an African province developed engine trouble and was forced to make an emergency landing. No one was seriously injured, but the trauma of being surrounded by pygmies made them feel very uncomfortable. In order to survive, those who were on the plane had to convince the natives that they meant them no harm. Since they could not communicate through written or spoken language, how might this be accomplished?

- A shanty town in northern California became the temporary home for seventy-five migrant workers. The work force was composed of Haitian and Cambodian refugees who spoke only their native languages. How might the two groups communicate successfully?

DECISION-MAKING PROCESSES

- Inhabitants of a small town in Texas are experiencing a dramatic increase in certain diseases. The source of the problem has been traced to ineffective garbage collection and disposal procedures. In some sections of the town, garbage has remained on the streets for two weeks. Since there is no town government, how can decisions to bring about improvements be made?

- Three girls are spending the weekend together at a motel. There is one television set in the room, and each girl wants to view programs airing on different networks. Since their favorite shows come on at the same time, how can they decide which network to watch?

CONFLICT RESOLUTION

- Threats of physical violence have been directed toward a black family which recently moved into a previously all white community. While things have gone smoothly at school for the two sons, both have suffered much verbal abuse on the weekends. This potentially explosive situation has resulted in several meetings by small groups of residents. You have been asked to serve as a consultant to the president of the neighborhood association. What measures would you recommend to bring about a resolution that could satisfy all parties?

- You are a new enrollee in a school where children who do not conform are treated with contempt by a large portion of the student body. Individuals who are obviously different experience the brunt of this inhumane treatment. As one who is ethnically, economically, and racially different from the majority of the school's population, you have been subjected to much verbal abuse. You have been told by your parents that some kind of retaliation is necessary. What suggestions for a peaceful resolution can you offer?

COUNTING AND MEASURING

- A family of nine people received a donation of thirteen ears of corn which will become its evening meal. What suggestions would you have for dividing the corn equally among the family members?

- A farmer, who never learned to count, has the feeling that the number of cattle on his farm is decreasing. How can he decide if the number remains constant from this point on?

CONSUMER ECONOMICS

- What kind of information is needed to help decide whether to make major food purchases from the neighborhood grocer or from one of the large supermarkets?

- The demand for coal has fallen, and the supply has increased during the past twenty years. Considering these two factors, why has the price of coal gone up?

HEALTH AND SAFETY

- You are responsible for the over-night safety of six young children whose ages range from four to nine years. As a teenager with no formal training in childcare, you must rely on your own resourcefulness. A blizzard has caused an electrical power failure; traffic cannot move because of the drifting snow, and the outside temperature is approaching ten degrees below zero. With the temperature inside the two-bedroom apartment falling rapidly, what steps might be taken to keep the children warm?

- You are lost in the wilderness and must rely on the different kinds of vegetation for survival. How might you decide on what could be consumed safely?

These exercises in creative problem solving provide lots of information regarding students' pre-existing knowledge, their use of thought processes, and their ability to analyze problem situations. More importantly, they make students aware that their prior knowledge can be utilized in new learning experiences. Armed with this kind of information, the teacher's task of relating what is about to be taught to what students already know is facilitated greatly.

Let's assume that you are introducing a unit on fire prevention. Because you had your class engage in a creative problem solving exercise you are now aware that while most of the students were familiar with many precautions that can prevent fires, there were several who expressed ideas about what should be done in case of fire that differed from the majority. One girl whose father was a forest ranger had learned that fires could be extinguished, or at least controlled, by setting "backfires." What this method accomplishes is to reduce the fire's fuel supply. Once the fire has consumed all of the fuel available, it extinguishes itself. Another student whose mother was a chef had learned that fire may be extinguished if it were covered with a fire blanket. This procedure reduces the supply of oxygen available to support combustion. However, most of the children knew that fires could be put out with water or with commercial fire extinguishers.

Further analysis of all these methods will lead students to the understanding that there are three ingredients essential for maintaining combustion. Each of these ingredients, FUEL, OXYGEN, and HEAT, must be present in sufficient quantity. Removal of either, a combination of any two or all three form the most common approaches for fighting fires.

By taking full advantage of what each student already knows, the learning experience is enhanced for all.

Every student present should come to the realization that the process of fighting fire with fire is another way of reducing the fire's fuel supply or that the use of a fire blanket reduces the amount of oxygen needed to support combustion. They will see also that the use of water and most commercial fire extinguishers serve to lower temperature as well as reduce the oxygen supply. When strategies similar to those being described herein are utilized by teachers, education that is truly multicultural takes place. Learning outcomes for all students are increased, and their appreciation for cultural differences is easily discernible.

CHAPTER FIVE

SUSTAINING INTEREST

Many educators have recognized that much of the subject matter taught in schools is somewhat less than captivating. When presented unembellished, it can become a painful experience for both students and teachers. Fortunately, or unfortunately, decisions regarding what should be taught at the various levels of schooling have been removed from the discretion of building-level practitioners. Thus, inducing learning of concepts that hold little enchantment for students remains as one of the unique responsibilities of those who dare to teach.

From a student perspective, boredom and the ability to predict accurately what will transpire in the classroom are mutually reinforcing. This would seem to suggest that reducing predictability would, at the very least, stimulate curiosity. When properly nurtured, curiosity can be transformed into genuine enthusiasm. This philosophy is similar to that which guides Spielberg's efforts in motion picture productions.

One strategy for reducing the ability of students to predict what will take place in the classroom is the use of counter-intuitive interventions. By definition, things which fall into this category defy immediate comprehension by most students, but are not incomprehensible. Selections from Ripley's "Believe It or Not," optical illusions created by mirrors or straight lines, perpetual motion displays, dancing mothballs in a solution of vinegar and water, and creative uses of the center of gravity for balance are examples of the kinds of things that work well. They are available in such abundance that little effort is required to find appropriate matches for given lessons.

The concept, "teachable moment," is one that is embraced by all who labor in this profession. When used to its fullest advantage, the benefits that accrue to students are irrefutable. A new concept, "critical moment," may be defined as any of the specific periods during a lesson when the use of or reference to appropriate counter-intuitive events or ideas would have its greatest impact. Using them at pre-determined times leads to predictability.

The following examples are presented to facilitate implementation. Since this can be accomplished in science and math rather effortlessly, other subject areas will receive the major focus.

EXAMPLES FOR USE IN ENGLISH

It is important to understand that counter-intuitive interventions are not restricted to weird or unusual phenomena. To qualify as such, events or ideas need only to defy immediate comprehension on initial exposure to students. At a critical moment during a lesson designed to raise students' levels of competence in subject/verb agreement, the concepts of ideal and grammatical subjects may be introduced. These concepts are extremely valuable in helping students select the proper verb in sentences such as:

- The box of cookies (is, are) on the table.

- Each of the girls (was, were) on time.

- Slices of cake (was, were) falling from the truck.

Ideal Subject: The ideal subject of a sentence is its primary reference or focus.

Grammatical Subject: The grammatical subject of a sentence is the word or words that must enter into agreement with the verb.

Selection of the correct verb is compounded for students in those sentences where the ideal and grammatical subjects are different words. Let's examine those examples more closely.

- The box of cookies (is, are) on the table.

In this sentence, the ideal subject is cookies. However, the grammatical subject which must enter into agreement with the verb is box. Therefore, the correct verb would be <u>is</u>.

- Each of the girls (was, were) on time.

In this sentence, the ideal subject is girls and the grammatical subject is each. Since each is singular, the correct verb would be <u>was</u>.

- Slices of cake (was, were) falling from the truck.

In this sentence, the ideal subject is cake, and the grammatical subject is slices. Therefore, the correct verb would be <u>were</u>.

Another critical moment may arise during a lesson designed to raise students' levels of competence in syntactical thought. Place the following sentence on the chalkboard:

- The dogs looked longer than the cats.

Ask various students to explain the message you are trying to convey. Some interesting responses should ensue. Since you have deliberately constructed a sentence that is structurally ambiguous, the students have no way of extracting a precise meaning. Lead them to discover that the use of the word <u>longer</u>, in this context, gives rise to ambiguity. There are insufficient signals to determine accurately whether <u>longer</u> implies comparisons of size or time spent in search of something.

At another critical moment, the linguistic concept dealing with classes of words may be introduced. Linguistically, these classes of words function in much the same manner as conventional parts of speech. However, a major difference lies in how each is defined. The difference in definitions makes, for some, interesting debate regarding classification. The linguistic counterpart for conventional adjectives is Class III Words. While adjectives are defined by function, Class III Words are defined in accordance with the affixes and inflections they can accommodate. A comparison of those definitions follows:

Adjectives: Adjectives are words that modify or describe nouns, pronouns, or other adjectives.

Class III Words: Pure adjectives are words having a base form that can take inflections in /-er/ and /-est/.

This interesting contrast emerges with attempts at classifying the word brick in the following sentence:

- A brick wall separated the two yards.

Conventionally, brick is an adjective modifying the noun, wall. Linguistically, brick can never be an adjective because it cannot accept inflections in /-er/ and /-est/. It is a noun modifying another noun; more specifically, brick wall is a noun adjunct.

Teachers who elect to use some of these linguistic concepts, should never lose sight of the intended purpose. Whether students conclude that brick is an adjective or a noun is of little consequence. The importance of this exercise arises from the dichotomy in thought processes used in classification. It is the dichotomy of thought that satisfies the requirements of counter-intuitive interventions. Activities such as these sustain interest while enhancing motivation to achieve.

EXAMPLES FOR USE IN READING

Whether reading is taught through content fields, language experience, or basal texts, opportunities for counter-intuitive interventions are extensive. The number of alien concepts introduced magnifies what is sometimes referred to as attention deficit syndrome or inability to attend. In many children, this phenomenon is more often a product of their changing interests, or their lack of interest in a particular topic than the result of any neurological dysfunction. Critical moments arise more frequently during the teaching of reading than any of the other subject areas. While the precise reason for this is not clear, it is clear that inattentiveness is reduced significantly by the use of counter-intuitive interventions.

Another linguistic concept that may be introduced during one of those critical moments is the definition of word. Linguistically, word is defined as a group of phonemes pronounced without juncture and having a meaning. Obviously, this definition raises questions about the concept of multiple meanings. Nelson Francis, a linguist of considerable stature, suggests that to perceive a word as having multiple meanings is to destroy the notion of word itself. He maintains that meaning serves to distinguish one word from another. In order to facilitate student understanding of this concept, the problem of homophony must be resolved. Homophones are words having the same sound but different meanings. They are more readily recognized as such in words like <u>to</u>, <u>too</u>, and <u>two</u> where the spellings are different. However, in the following sentences, three homophones, written and pronounced identically, are being used.

- An elephant breathes through its <u>trunk</u>.

- Several packages were placed in the <u>trunk</u> of the automobile.

- Bark from the <u>trunk</u> of a tree was used to keep the fire burning.

In each of these sentences, <u>trunk</u> has a different meaning. When the meanings are different, the words to which those meanings are ascribed are different.

The notion that distinctions among words are based on spellings and pronunciations can be shattered through several approaches. One logical approach rests on the proposition of identical qualities. This proposition suggests that words which are identical should be able to accommodate identical affixes. Let's examine the examples below:

- The bell will <u>ring</u> in five minutes.

- This <u>ring</u> is too small for my finger.

The word <u>ring</u> used in the first example can accommodate /-ing/.

- The bell will be <u>ringing</u> in five minutes.

53

Clearly, this is not the case with the word <u>ring</u> in the second example. Some students will accept the linguistic concept of word and others will not. Regardless of their acceptance or rejection, the purpose served by its introduction is no less valuable.

During another critical moment, the linguistic concept of compound words may be explored. Linguistically, words are identified as compounds not by their graphic representations, but rather by the stress patterns used in pronunciation. The supra-segmental phonemes of pitch, stress, and juncture are not always indicated by graphics. Thus, <u>horse</u> <u>fly</u> and <u>green</u> <u>house</u> are distinguished from <u>horsefly</u> and <u>greenhouse</u> by the stress patterns and the use of juncture in pronunciation. It should be pointed out that not all compounds are written as one word. Those that are not represented graphically as compounds may be identified as such through pronunciation.

Example: The carpenter <u>looked</u> <u>over</u> the fence.

When the words <u>looked</u> <u>over</u> are pronounced with juncture and primary stress on each, the message conveyed refers to the carpenter's field of vision or line of sight. However, if the pronunciation of <u>looked</u> <u>over</u> utilizes the primary/secondary stress pattern and is without juncture, the message conveyed is the carpenter examined or inspected the fence. The graphic representations are identical, but the meanings conveyed are quite different.

Still another critical moment may be filled by processing a short reading selection. The reproduction should contain no signals that would allow students to isolate individual sentences. After time for mental processing, have volunteers share with the class whatever meaning they have extracted. The results are fascinating,

EXAMPLES FOR USE IN SOCIAL STUDIES

Because of its emphasis on history and geography, embellishment of social studies lessons is essential in preventing boredom. References to people, places, dates, and events form the very essence of this curriculum. Student retention of the information presented is increased dramatically by the frequent use of counter-intuitive interventions.

The use of absurd analogies is particularly appropriate for this area. These analogies are characterized as absurd because of their apparent lack of similar qualities. The key to using them successfully is in having students identify the similarities that exist. During a critical moment in your lesson, you might have individuals respond to such questions as:

- How is a country similar to an airport?

- How is socialized medicine similar to a kidney?

- How is an anarchy similar to a social studies class?

These kinds of questions demand a type of originality in thought seldom required in student responses. In each analogy used, part of it should deal with a concept related to the social studies curriculum. Engaging in this kind of exercise renews interest for the students and broadens their understanding of important concepts.

Another kind of counter-intuitive intervention involves the use of pictures, charts, and graphs which present factual information that runs counter to popular beliefs. Magazines and newspapers are excellent sources from which an adequate supply of these materials may be obtained. At a critical moment during a lesson, you might display the traditional artist's conception of Washington Crossing the Delaware. Allow one minute for students to concentrate on the details; remove the visual from view, and ask if there were any minorities represented in the boat. Most of the students in the class will not notice the minorities simply because their presence was not anticipated. In addition to sustaining interest, this kind of activity helps students become more objective observers.

Another type of counter-intuitive intervention involves having students decipher various concepts represented through unconventional means such as "Wuzzles." Wuzzles, created by Tom Underwood and syndicated in newspapers across the country, are familiar concepts represented by a special relationship of other words or symbols to each other.

Examples:
(noon Saturday) = Saturday afternoon

(mind)
(matter)   = mind over matter

(day day)   = day after day

(church/state)   = separation between
                     church and state

Since many of the concepts presented through the social studies curriculum do not lend themselves to this kind of strategy, limited use serves to increase its effectiveness.

A final example of another excellent strategy for sustaining interest is reinactments of historical events. Although not classified as counter-intuitive, students respond enthusiastically to their use. Events such as the Burr-Hamilton duel, the assassination of Lincoln, the resignation of Richard Nixon, and the Gibraltar summit may be reinacted by small groups of students. These reinactments are extremely effective when they are planned and presented with minimal teacher involvement. With a student committee making most of the decisions, brief reinactments can occur on a weekly basis.

The one thing that can be said with certainty regarding the use of counter-intuitive interventions is that they are instrumental in sustaining interest in the learning process. If they accomplish no other purpose, the time and energy required for implementation is a wise investment. Because they are, in most cases, both pedagogically sound and aesthetically appealing, many other benefits accrue from their use. Teachers who are convinced of those benefits will find creative ways to incorporate them in their lessons.

CHAPTER SIX

SOME FINAL COMMENTS

Each of the preceeding chapters has dealt with several critical issues associated with the teaching endeavor. These issues, when handled inappropriately by teachers, combine to limit academic growth for many students, particularly minorities. Unfortunately, this marginal rate of growth is perceived often by educational practitioners as resulting from students' lack of motivation to achieve. Because the problem of minority underachievement is seen as originating with the students, adequate efforts to analyze and modify the delivery of instructional services have not been made.

When academically able students are making only marginal progress in our schools, more than students' motivation to achieve needs to be questioned. We should feel compelled to examine the impact on learning produced by our educational exchanges with youth. If teachers concentrate only on the issues addressed in this handbook, the benefits for students should be immeasurable.

Probably the most important attribute of this entire effort is its potential to produce incredible results from a limited amount of educational reform. How students react to and participate in the learning process are influenced tremendously when teachers invest the time and energy to deal effectively with the following:

- Establishing an Atmosphere of Mutual Respect

- Establishing a Need to Know

- Discovering What Students Already Know

- Sustaining Interest

The true test of how effectively these issues have been handled must be measured in terms of student achievement. Peter Drucker suggests that efficiency results from doing things right, while effectiveness results from doing the right things. The number of minority students experiencing academic failure indicates clearly that we are not doing the right things. In order to change the present situation, we must engage continuously in critical self-analyses. Any efforts directed toward that end are enhanced significantly by video taping and critiqueing lesson segments.

As teachers grow in experience and confidence, the likelihood of their teaching intuitively increases. Intuitive teaching and critical self-analysis are mutually exclusive events. These limitations to introspection prevail partially because decisions about teaching are made without substantial forethought and partially because those decisions result in teaching behaviors that cannot be recalled. Without improvements that arise from the self-criticisms of individual teachers, the state of minority achievement will remain impervious to change. At the risk of overstating the importance of analyzing the impact of teaching on students' motivation to achieve, let's examine the following vignette:

> Miss Brown, an extremely conscientious individual in her seventh year of teaching English at an inner-city high school, was distressed over the inappropriate behavior displayed by several students in each of her classes. These behaviors surfaced invariably when she wrote on the chalkboard with her back to the class. Rapid glances calculated to identify the guilty parties were unsuccessful. With each occurrence, she tried more desperately to catch those responsible for the disruptions. Knowing the loyalties students held for one another, she understood fully why no one came forth with information about the offenders.
>
> Determined to rely on her own resourcefulness, this young teacher decided to set up a video camera in the rear of the classroom. Since no monitor was connected, the students assumed that

the unit would be used for a future activity. After the fourth day, they became oblivious to its presence.

On Monday of the following week, Miss Brown taped her third period class. Of all her classes, this one had caused the most grief. When it became necessary for her to write on the chalkboard, the disruptive behaviors occurred on cue. This teacher's obvious determination to catch someone misbehaving resulted in several students' becoming even more devious to escape detection. Predictably in this kind of struggle, the students were the winners.

At the end of the day, Miss Brown's critique of the tape became an invaluable learning experience. What she found to be most revealing were the nonverbal messages being conveyed by her own behaviors. Those messages could be perceived only as encouraging rather than discouraging the kinds of disruptions that ensued. It was clear to Miss Brown that those students involved viewed her attempts to catch them as a challenge to their ability to avoid being caught. There were no signals suggesting that inappropriate behavior would not be tolerated.

From that point on, Miss Brown reacted to disruptions that occurred while

she was writing on the board by deliberately turning slowly to face the class.
She would stare purposefully, but say
nothing. The message conveyed was
clear, and the displays of inappropriate
behaviors were reduced significantly.

If the teaching profession is to be accorded the
prominence it deserves, then the effectiveness of individual teachers will have to be enhanced. Miss Brown's will-
ingness to examine her own behavior greatly increased
her effectiveness as a teacher. There is no substitute for
critical self-analysis. As an access route toward improved
performance, this road should be traveled frequently by
those who dare to teach.

Because many of the inequities minorities encounter
in schools are imposed unwittingly by teachers, critical
self-analyses must focus on subtleties as well as those
areas assumed to be well defined. Chapter Two advanced five postulates on which the underlying rationale
for all of the ideas presented in this handbook are based.
As you engage in self-critiques, those postulates can serve
as a frame of reference against which some of your teaching behaviors may be judged.

SELF-ASSESSMENT OF CRITICAL TEACHING
 BEHAVIORS

If all of the following questions can be answered in
the affirmative, you are one of those truly exceptional
teachers who brings credit to the entire profession.

1. TEACHING IS INTERACTION THAT
   FACILITATES LEARNING.

- Do I challenge all students with questions that stimulate higher-level thought processes?

- Do I expect all students to perform at levels commensurate with their potential?

- Do I provide appropriate wait time for all students?

- Do I use proximity influence and control with all students?

- Do I provide feedback to all students that is appropriate, specific, and sincere?

- Do I introduce new units of study by a process which allows each student to see the connections between the skills to be taught and how he/she lives?

- Do I allow all students to establish their own purposes for learning?

- Do I spend sufficient time on the introductory process to ensure that all students have made those connections?

- Do I take full advantage of what students already know?

- Do I check frequently for student understanding?

- Do I connect statements about behavior to learning goals?

2. DIFFERENCES SHOULD NOT ONLY BE TOLERATED, THEY MUST BE AFFIRMED.

- Do I recognize differences as serving the purpose of making distinctions rather than determining inherent worth?

- Do I recognize that while all students can learn the same things, they learn for different reasons?

- Do I recognize that students learn in a variety of ways?

- Do I recognize that acquisition of the same skills affects the lives of different students in different ways?

- Do I recognize that while the impact of learning experiences may differ, those differences are of equal importance to the learners?

- Do I dignify student responses that are inconsistent with facts or what I believe to be true?

- Do I refrain from demeaning behaviors that I find inappropriate?

- Do I view variant dialects of English as legitimate means of communicating?

3. VALUES ARE NEITHER RIGHT NOR WRONG; THEY SIMPLY EXIST IN ALL OF US

- Do I treat values that differ from my own as though they have emerged from conscious choices?

- Do I recognize that values form the basis for many real-life decisions?

- Do my efforts to instill different values include presenting many options to be accepted or rejected through student analyses of benefits and consequences?

- Do I refrain from moralizing about behaviors that offend me?

- Do I refrain from deriding behaviors and beliefs that differ from my own?

4. THE RIGHT TO CHOOSE IS ONE OF THE MOST PRECIOUS RIGHTS WE HAVE.

- Does my behavior reflect the belief that students have the right to exercise freedom of choice?

- Does my behavior reflect the belief that encouraging students to analyze consequences invites the making of more appropriate choices?

- Does my behavior reflect the belief that attempts to force conformance are open invitations for defiance?

- Does my behavior reflect a desire to avoid power struggles?

5. THOSE WHO DARE TO TEACH MUST NEVER CEASE TO LEARN.

- Do I seek information about minority cultures and subcultures from all available sources?

- Do I verify the information obtained to form a knowledge base?

- Do I use that knowledge base to modify many of my teaching behaviors?

Behaviors related to these thirty questions are, in most instances, representative of the differential kinds of treatment that account for disparity in achievement levels among racially, ethnically, and economically diverse populations. Each deals with student/teacher interaction. Remember, IF WE CAN'T INTERACT WITH THEM, WE CAN'T TEACH THEM.

SUGGESTED READINGS

Arnez, N.L. "Implications of Desegregation as a Discriminatory Process," Journal of Negro Education, XLII (1987), 28-45.

Bloom, B.S. "Talent Development vs. Schooling," Educational Leadership, XXXIX (November, 1981), 86-94.

Boyer, J.B. Multicultural Education: Product or Process, Kansas City, KS: Kansas Urban Education Center, 1985.

Brown, T.J. and O. Taylor. "Should Black English Be Taught in Elementary Schools?" Instructor, LXXXIX (April, 1980), 22.

Brown, T.J. Teaching Minorities More Effectively: A Model for Educators, Lanham, MD: University Press of America, Inc., 1986.

Cheyney, A.B. Teaching Culturally Disadvantaged in the Elementary Schools, Columbus, OH: Merrill Publishing Co., 1967.

Comer, J.P. "Black Children in a Racist Society," Current, CLXII (May, 1974), 53-56.

Cooper, H.M. and T.L. Good, Pygmalion Grows Up, New York: Longman, Inc., 1982.

Crain, R.L. and R. Mahard. "Desegregation and Black Achievement," Law and Contemporary Problems, LXII (1987), 17-56.

Crain, R.L. and R. Mahard. "Some Policy Implications of the Desegregation Minority Achievement Literature," In Hawley, W.D. Assessment of the Current Knowledge about the Effectiveness of School Desegregation Strategies. Nashville: Vanderbilt University, Institute for Public Policy Studies, Center for Education and Human Development, 1981.

Crowl, T.K. "White Teachers' Evaluation of Oral Responses Given by White and Negro Ninth Grade Males," Dissertation Abstracts, 3 (1971: 4540a).

Denbo, S. Improving Minority Student Achievement: Focus on the Classroom, Washington, DC: The Mid-Atlantic Center for Race Equity, 1986.

Edelman, M.W. Portrait of Inequality: Black and White Children in America, Washington, DC: Washington Research Project, 1980.

Epps, E.C. "The Impact of School Desegregation on the Self-Evaluation and Achievement Orientation of Minority Children," Law and Contemporary Problems, XLII (Summer, 1978), 57-76.

Epps, E.C. Cultural Pluralism, California: McCutchan Publishing Corporation, 1974.

Finley, D. "Why Eskimo Education Isn't Working," Phi Delta Kappan, LXIV (April, 1983), 580-581.

Fordham, S. and J. Ogbu. "Black Students' School Success: Coping with the Burden of Acting White," Urban Review, XVIII (Spring, 1986), 176-206.

Good, T.L. "Teacher Expectations and Student Perceptions: A Decade of Research," Educational Leadership, XXXVIII (April, 1981), 415-422.

Good, T.L. and J.E. Brophy. "Analyzing Classroom Interaction: A More Powerful Alternative." Educational Technology, XI (October, 1971), 36.

Hale, J.E. Black Children: Their Roots, Culture and Learning Styles, New York: Brigham Press, 1982.

Hall, L. "Race and Suspension: A Second General Desegregation Problem," In Moody, C.D., J. William and C.B. Vergen Ed., Student Rights and Discipline, Ann Arbor: University of Michigan School of Law, 1978.

Hilliard, A.G., III. "Cultural Diversity and Special Education," Exceptional Children, XLVI (May, 1980), 584-588.

Hollins, E.R. "The Marva Collins Story Revisited: Implications for Regular Classroom Instruction," Journal of Teacher Education, XXXIII (January-February, 1982), 37-40.

Howard, B. Learning to Persist/Persisting to Learn, Washington, DC: The Mid-Atlantic Center for Race Equity, The American University, 1986.

Kunjufu, J. Countering the Conspiracy to Destroy Black Boys, Chicago: African American Images, 1985.

Kunjufu, J. Countering the Conspiracy to Destry Black Boys, Volume II, Chicago: African American Images, 1986.

Leacock, E. Teaching and Learning in City Schools: A Comparative Study, New York: Basic Books, 1969.

Morgan, H. "How Schools Fail Black Children," Social Policy, X (January-February, 1980), 49-54.

Rist, R.C. "Student Social Class and Teacher Expectation: The Self-Fulfilling Prophecy in Ghetto Education," Harvard Educational Review, XL (1970), 411-415.

Rubovitz, P.C. and M. Maehr. "Pygmalion Black and White," Journal of Personality and Social Psychology, XXV (1973), 210.

Smith, E. Black Students in Interracial Schools: A Guide for Students, Teachers, and Parents, Garrett Park, MD: Garrett Park Press, 1980.

Smith, G.P. "The Critical Issue of Excellence and Equity in Competency Testing," Journal of Teacher Education, XXXV (March-April, 1984), 6-9.

Staples, R. Black Masculinity, San Francisco: The Black Scholar Press, 1982.

Stodolsky, S. and G. Lesser. "Learning Patterns in the Disadvantaged," Harvard Educational Review, XXXVII (Fall, 1967), 546-593.

Taylor, O.L. "An Introduction to the Historical Development of Black English," Language, Speech, and Hearing Services in Schools, III (October, 1972), 5-15.

Thomas, D.M. "The Limits of Pluralism," Phi Delta Kappan, LXII (April, 1981), 589-591.

VanBrunt, V., Ed. Black Students in a Multicultural Setting: Implications for Teacher Effectiveness, Madison, WI: Institute for Cultural Pluralism, The University of Wisconsin, 1979.

Woodworth, W.P. and R.T. Salzer. "Black Children's Speech and Teacher Evaluation," Urban Education, VI (July, 1971), 167-173.